W9-CAL-045

MERCURY

by Ruth Owen

WINDMILL
BOOKS
NEW YORK

Published in 2014 by Windmill Books, An Imprint of Rosen Publishing
29 East 21st Street, New York, NY 10010

Produced for Windmill by Ruby Tuesday Books Ltd
Editor for Ruby Tuesday Books Ltd: Mark J. Sachner
US Editor: Sara Howell
Designer: Emma Randall
Consultant: Kevin Yates, Fellow of the Royal Astronomical Society

Photo Credits:
Cover, 1, 9, 11, 12–13, 19 (top), 19 (bottom), 20–21, 23, 24–25, 26–27 © NASA; 4, 10 © Wikipedia Creative Commons; 5, 7, 8, 17 (top), 18–19, 28–29 © Shutterstock; 14–15 © Science Photo Library; 15 (bottom) © Ruby Tuesday Books; 16–17 © European Southern Observatory.

Library of Congress Cataloging-in-Publication Data

Owen, Ruth, 1967–
 Mercury / by Ruth Owen.
   p. cm. — (Explore outer space)
 Includes index.
 ISBN 978-1-61533-722-4 (library binding) — ISBN 978-1-61533-761-3 (pbk.) —
 ISBN 978-1-61533-762-0 (6-pack)
 1. Mercury (Planet)—Juvenile literature. 2. Mercury (Planet)—Exploration—Juvenile literature. I. Title. II. Series: Owen, Ruth, 1967– Explore outer space.
 QB611.O93 2014
 523.41—dc23
                                         2013003828

Manufactured in the United States of America

CPSIA Compliance Information: Batch #BS13WM: For Further Information contact Windmill Books, New York, New York at 1-866-478-0556

CONTENTS

THE SUN'S TINY NEIGHBOR

Many millions of miles (km) from Earth is a battered, sun-scorched world called Mercury. This tiny **planet** is **orbiting** the Sun at an average speed of 31 miles per second (48 km/s).

From Earth, the Sun is a warming yellowish-white ball of light in the sky. From the surface of Mercury it's a very different story, because Mercury is the closest planet to the Sun. If you could stand on Mercury's surface during the part of its orbit when it is closest to the Sun, the Sun would appear three times larger than it does from Earth and over 10 times brighter! If you were standing on Mercury during the day, you would experience a scorching heat of 800 °F (427 °C).

Mercury is the smallest planet in the **solar system** and is only slightly larger than Earth's moon. If you can imagine the Earth as a baseball, little Mercury, by comparison, is just the size of a golf ball.

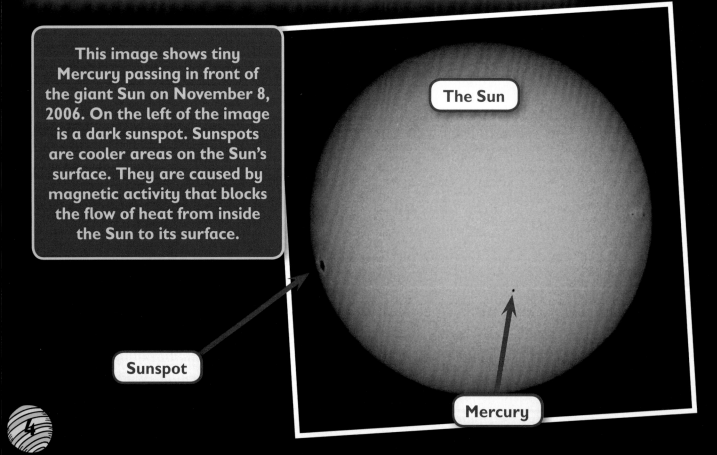

This image shows tiny Mercury passing in front of the giant Sun on November 8, 2006. On the left of the image is a dark sunspot. Sunspots are cooler areas on the Sun's surface. They are caused by magnetic activity that blocks the flow of heat from inside the Sun to its surface.

The Sun

Sunspot

Mercury

That's Out of This World!

Thirteen times every century Mercury can be seen from Earth passing across the face of the Sun. This is called a **transit**. People should never look directly at the Sun, because the Sun's light will seriously damage their eyes. It's possible to see a transit, however, in pictures that have been captured by special **astronomy** equipment.

THE BIRTH OF A PLANET

About five billion years ago, Mercury did not exist. Earth, Mars, all the other planets in our solar system, and even the Sun were yet to be born.

The chemical ingredients to make the Sun and everything in the solar system did exist, though. These ingredients were floating in space in a **nebula**, which is a cloud of gas and dust.

Then, part of the cloud began to collapse on itself, forming a massive rotating sphere, or ball. A disk formed around the sphere from the remaining gas and dust. The material in the sphere was pressed together by **gravity**, causing pressure to build. As pressure built, the sphere's core heated up, reaching temperatures of around 18 million°F (10 million°C). Finally, the heat and pressure became so great that the sphere ignited, and a star was born. This new star was our Sun.

Gas and dust continued to spin in a disk around the newly-formed star. Over time, this material clumped together, forming Mercury, Earth, and all the other planets and objects in the solar system.

That's Out of This World!

Nebulae are the places where stars form.
They are often called "star factories" or "star nurseries."
These clouds of gas and dust can be different shapes and
colors, and are trillions of miles (km) wide.

This illustration shows gas and dust clumping together to form a new planet.

A planet forming

Spinning gas and dust

Rock forming from gas and dust

Imagining The Solar System

From our position here on Earth, it can be hard to imagine the vastness of our solar system. There is a fun way, however, to experience the scale of the solar system and visualize the size of the planets in comparison with each other.

If you take a bowling ball and imagine that it is the Sun, then small planets such as Mercury and Mars and the **dwarf planet** Pluto could be represented by pinheads. Venus and Earth would be the size of a peppercorn. Uranus and Neptune would be the size of a coffee bean, while Saturn would be marble-sized, and giant Jupiter the size of a chestnut.

To match the scaled-down dimensions of the solar system, tiny pinhead Mercury would be about 10 yards (9 m) from the bowling ball Sun. The peppercorn Venus would be 9 yards (8 m) past Mercury, and Earth would be 7 yards (6 m) past Venus. Keep going with Mars, Jupiter, Saturn, Uranus, and Neptune. Finally, pinhead Pluto would be located just over 1,000 yards (914 m) from the bowling ball Sun. That's about the same length as 10 football fields!

A pinhead = Mercury

A bowling ball = the Sun

8

This illustration shows the relative sizes of the solar system's eight planets and Pluto.

Mercury

Earth

Venus

Mars

Neptune

Uranus

Pluto

Jupiter

Saturn

That's Out of This World!

In actual space, Mercury has a diameter, or distance across, of 3,032 miles (4,880 km). The Sun's diameter, at 864,337 miles (1,391,016 km), is over 280 times greater than Mercury's.

Mercury, Inside And Out

Just like Earth, Mercury's inner structure is made up of three different layers.

Inside the planet is a huge core of iron that makes up about 80 percent of the planet's **mass**. The iron core is partially **molten** and has a radius of about 1,100 miles (1,800 km) from the center of the planet.

Surrounding the core is the mantle. This layer of molten rock is up to 400 miles (650 km) thick. The outer crust of the planet is a 180-mile-(300 km) thick layer of rock covered by gray rocks and dust.

Mercury has less mass than Earth, so the gravity on its surface is only about 38 percent of the gravity we experience on Earth. This means if you weigh 100 pounds (45 kg) on Earth, you would weigh only 38 pounds (17 kg) on Mercury.

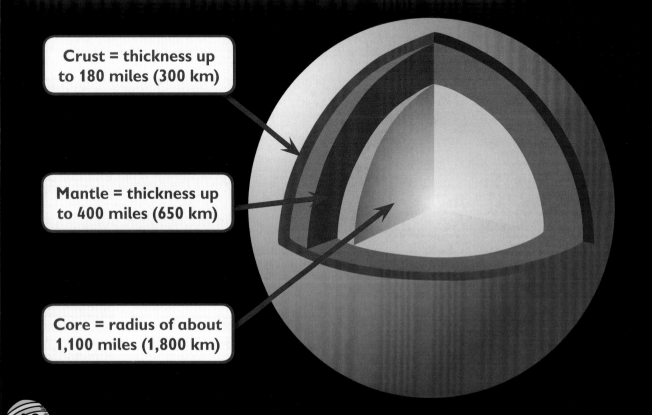

Crust = thickness up to 180 miles (300 km)

Mantle = thickness up to 400 miles (650 km)

Core = radius of about 1,100 miles (1,800 km)

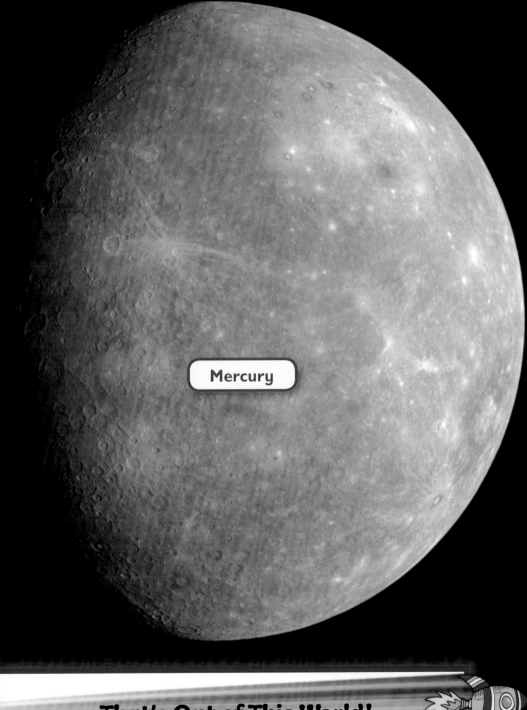

Mercury

That's Out of This World!

Mercury's circumference at its **equator** is 9,525 miles (15,329 km) around. If you drove a car at 60 miles per hour (97 km/h) day and night, it would take just under a week to drive around Mercury.

Black Skies And No Atmosphere

Our Earth is surrounded by a protective blanket of gases called the **atmosphere**. Mercury formed in the same way and at the same time as Earth, but Mercury has no atmosphere.

A planet's atmosphere is held in place by its gravity. The planet's gravitational force stops the gases from floating off into space. Little Mercury's low gravity made it difficult for the planet to hold onto an atmosphere in the way that the Earth has done.

Another factor in retaining an atmosphere is a planet's surface temperature. The hotter atmospheric gases become, the faster the gas **molecules** whiz around. Fast-moving gas molecules are even harder for a planet's gravity to hold in place!

Mercury's surface is extremely hot, so this combination of heat and low gravitational force meant that, unlike Earth, Mercury quickly lost most of its atmosphere.

That's Out of This World!

Mercury's closeness to the Sun and its lack of a protective atmosphere means that daytime surface temperatures reach 800 °F (427°C). With no atmosphere to store daytime heat, nighttime temperatures drop to -280 °F (−173°C).

12

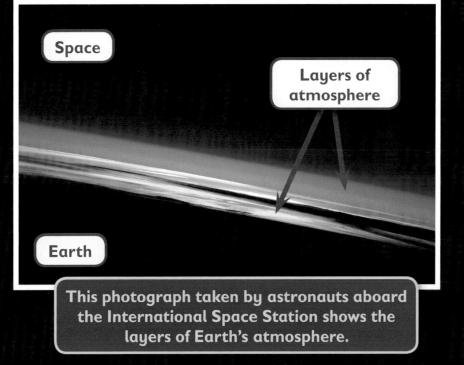

Space

Layers of atmosphere

Earth

This photograph taken by astronauts aboard the International Space Station shows the layers of Earth's atmosphere.

Mercury's horizon

On Earth, the atmosphere scatters the Sun's light, allowing mostly blue light waves through. This is why Earth's daytime sky looks blue. On Mercury, the lack of atmosphere means there is nothing but the blackness of space, day and night.

MERCURY'S DAYS AND YEARS

Earth orbits the Sun in a year, or once every 365 days. As it orbits, it also rotates on its **axis** once every 24 hours. We call this time period a day. Like Earth, Mercury also has years and days.

To orbit the Sun once, Earth must make a journey of nearly 560 million miles (900 million km). Because Mercury is much closer to the Sun, its journey is much shorter at 226 million miles (364 million km). Mercury is also a fast-moving planet. It travels through space at about 106,000 miles per hour (170,500 km/h), faster than Earth's speed of 67,000 miles per hour (107,000 km/h). This all adds up to Mercury making one orbit of the Sun every 88 days. So a year on Mercury is just 88 Earth days long.

Mercury, however, rotates on its own axis much slower than Earth. It takes Mercury nearly 59 Earth days to make just one rotation. So a day on Mercury lasts 59 days.

> The Sun

That's Out of This World!

Mercury's orbit of the Sun is elliptical, or oval-shaped, and its distance from the Sun varies as it moves through one orbit. At times Mercury is only 29 million miles (47 million km) from the Sun. At others, it is 43 million miles (70 million km) away.

14

This artwork shows the Sun rising over Mercury's rocky, barren surface.

Earth

Venus

Surface of Mercury

Mercury

Sun

This diagram shows Mercury's counterclockwise, elliptical orbit around the Sun.

Because Mercury can be seen in the sky with the naked eye, people have known about it for thousands of years.

From Earth, Mercury is visible just after sunset or just before sunrise. The ancient Greeks actually believed it was two different stars. They named the evening star Hermes, the Greek name for the god the Romans called Mercury. They named the morning star Apollo after the Greek god of music, healing, and the Sun. It wasn't until around 350 BC that ancient Greek **astronomers** realized Mercury was a single planet and not two stars.

In 1631, French astronomer Pierre Gassendi used a telescope to watch Mercury pass in front of the Sun. He was the first person to witness the transit of a planet across the Sun.

For centuries, astronomers watched Mercury from Earth through telescopes. Then, in 1973, a spacecraft blasted off from Earth that would bring the world incredible close-up images of the closest planet to the Sun.

Mercury

The Moon setting

This photograph shows an early morning sky in Chile. The Moon is setting, and Mercury and Venus can be seen in the sky.

A statue of Mercury

That's Out of This World!

The planets are named after Roman gods. Mercury was the Roman god of business, travel, and stealing. He is usually shown wearing a winged helmet and sandals. The planet Mercury probably got its name because, like the god, it moves quickly.

Mission to Mercury

On November 3, 1973, NASA's *Mariner 10* spacecraft blasted off from Cape Canaveral Air Force Station in Florida. The mission of the robotic spacecraft was to discover information about Venus and Mercury.

On February 5, 1974, *Mariner 10* flew past Venus, sending data and over 4,000 photos back to Earth. *Mariner 10* then used Venus's gravity to adjust its speed and **trajectory** so that it headed toward Mercury. It was the first spacecraft to use the gravity of one planet as a "slingshot" to assist its journey to another.

In March 1974, *Mariner 10* reached Mercury. The spacecraft made three flybys of the planet, taking photographs and collecting data. The photos it sent back to Earth showed a battered, rocky landscape not unlike the surface of the Moon. On March 24, 1975, with its mission complete, *Mariner 10*'s contact with Earth was shut down.

That's Out of This World!

Mariner 10's third and final flyby of Mercury was the closest. The spacecraft flew within 203 miles (327 km) of the planet. During its mission, *Mariner 10* sent back more than 7,000 images of Earth, the Moon, Venus, and Mercury.

This photograph shows *Mariner 10* and its range of instruments designed to study Mercury's atmosphere, surface, and physical characteristics.

his image is a mosaic, or combination, of many photographs tak by *Mariner 10*. It shows the southern hemisphere of Mercury.

MESSENGER

Nearly 30 years after *Mariner 10* blasted off for Mercury, another spacecraft left Earth heading for the little planet.

On August 3, 2004, *Messenger* was launched from Cape Canaveral Air Force Station in Florida. *Messenger*'s mission was to orbit Mercury and find out more about the planet's core, surface, and **geologic history**. On board the spacecraft were many scientific instruments for collecting data. *Messenger* was also fitted with **solar panels** to capture sunlight and use it to power the spacecraft. Solar power could also be stored in an onboard battery.

Mercury's earlier visitor, *Mariner 10*, was designed to fly by the planet. *Messenger*, however, would be orbiting the planet and experiencing the intense heat of the Sun for a long period of time. In order to enable the spacecraft to operate in the extreme temperatures close to Mercury, *Messenger* was fitted with a protective sunshade.

Both powered by and protected from the Sun, *Messenger* left Earth's atmosphere ready to continue the work begun by *Mariner 10* three decades before.

Messenger blasts off for Mercury on a Delta II rocket.

That's Out of This World!

Messenger's name was created from the scientific goals of the mission. It stands for "MErcury Surface, Space ENvironment, GEochemistry, and Ranging" (ranging is the process of bouncing laser beams off a surface to obtain a 3D image). The Roman god Mercury is also known as "the winged messenger."

Sunshade

Messenger

Solar panels

This picture combines an illustration of *Messenger* with an image of Mercury's surface as captured by *Messenger*. The colors on Mercury have been added by computer to make the planet's surface features easier to view.

Incredible Journey, Amazing Discoveries

Reaching Mercury and then entering into orbit around the planet required that *Messenger* make a long and complex journey.

As *Messenger* got closer to Mercury and its giant neighbor the Sun, the Sun's powerful gravity would cause the spacecraft to accelerate faster and faster. *Messenger* had to slow down enough to match Mercury's speed and allow the planet's weak gravity to capture it and pull it into orbit. In order to achieve the right speed and trajectory, *Messenger* had to make two flybys of Venus and then three flybys of Mercury. This complicated journey took six and a half years, but finally, in March 2011, *Messenger* went into orbit around Mercury.

Mariner 10 had captured images of about 45 percent of the planet's surface. One of *Messenger's* goals was to send back imagery of places not seen before. Now, thanks to *Messenger*, we've been able to see incredible images of huge cliffs, craters, and vast, deep impact basins caused by objects from space crashing into the planet.

That's Out of This World!

On the surface of Mercury there are many steep cliffs, known as rupes. These cliffs can stretch for hundreds of miles (km). Scientists believe Mercury's rupes formed in the early days of the planet. As Mercury's hot interior cooled and shrank, it caused the outer crust to contract and buckle, creating vast folds in the planet's surface.

This illustration shows one of Mercury's rupes.
These huge cliffs can be 1 mile (1.6 km) high!

Rupes

Craters

Victoria Rupes

This image was captured by *Messenger*.
It shows Victoria Rupes, a long cliff on Mercury.

MERCURY UNDER ATTACK!

Almost since it formed about 4.6 billion years ago, Mercury has been bombarded by asteroids, meteoroids, and comets.

It's the same for all the planets in the solar system. They all regularly collide with both small and massive chunks of space debris. Mercury, however, has no protective atmosphere to shield it from these impacts. When small objects such as meteoroids head for Earth, they burn up in our atmosphere or our atmosphere causes them to break into smaller, less damaging pieces. On Mercury, they hit the planet's surface intact and at full speed!

Billions of years of impacts have left Mercury's surface covered with small craters, large craters, and truly vast craters, known as impact basins.

Mercury is home to one of the solar system's largest impact basins, the Caloris Basin. This huge feature on the planet's surface was formed early in Mercury's life, when it was hit by a giant asteroid.

This *Messenger* image shows the Rembrandt impact basin, which was discovered by *Messenger* in October 2008. In addition to the main basin, it's possible to see many craters of different sizes.

Caloris Basin

That's Out of This World!

Mercury's giant impact basin, the Caloris Basin, has a diameter of about 930 miles (1,500 km).

DISCOVERING WATER ON MERCURY

One of *Messenger*'s most amazing discoveries was the presence of ice on Mercury.

When scientists on Earth bounced radio waves off Mercury, they saw unexpectedly bright reflections from some places on the planet's surface. They thought these bright areas could be a particularly reflective type of rock. Another theory, however, was that the bright areas were ice.

In 2011, instruments on board *Messenger* confirmed that these bright areas are indeed pure frozen water. In fact, there could be up to one trillion tons (907 billion t) of ice on the planet.

It seems unbelievable that ice could exist in one of the hottest places in the solar system. However, at the bottom of deep craters at Mercury's north and south poles, there are dark, extremely cold places that are never touched by the Sun's light and heat.

No one knows for sure how the ice came to be on Mercury. One theory is that it could have come from comets, which are mostly made of ice, that collided with the planet.

That's Out of This World!

One of the scientists on the *Messenger* team estimated that there is enough ice on Mercury to encase Washington, D.C., in a giant block of ice over 2 miles (3.2 km) deep!

MERCURY'S FINAL DAYS

Mercury will not be around forever. In about five billion years, little Mercury's life will likely come to an end!

Stars like our Sun may burn for billions of years. Eventually, however, their supply of fuel burns out. As the Sun's supply of hydrogen fuel runs out, the star will swell in size to become what is known as a red giant. As the Sun swells, its already vast diameter will actually increase by up to 250 times. As it swells, the Sun will swallow up Mercury, bringing its time in space to a fiery end. Mercury's nearest neighbors, Venus and Earth, will also be engulfed by the dying Sun.

After about a billion years, the Sun will begin to expel, or blow off, its outer layers. These layers of gas and dust will form a nebula. Finally, the remains of the Sun's core will collapse, leaving just a small, dense star called a white dwarf. Then, all the chemical ingredients that were once the Sun, Mercury, and its planetary neighbors will be floating in a giant cloud ready to become part of a new star or planet.

That's Out of This World!

Mercury, Venus, Earth, and Mars are called the terrestrial planets because they have solid, rocky surfaces. The word terrestrial comes from the Latin word *terra*, which means "earth" or "land."

Dying Sun

Mercury

GLOSSARY

asteroids (AS-teh-roydz)
Rocky objects orbiting the Sun and ranging in size from a few feet (m) to hundreds of miles (km) in diameter.

astronomers (uh-STRAH-nuh-merz)
Scientists who specialize in the study of outer space.

astronomy (uh-STRAH-nuh-mee)
The scientific study of outer space.

atmosphere (AT-muh-sfeer)
The layer of gases surrounding a planet, moon, or star.

axis (AK-sus)
An imaginary line about which a body, such as a planet, rotates.

comets (KAH-mits)
Objects orbiting the Sun consisting primarily of a nucleus, or center, of ice and dust and, when near the Sun, tails of gas and dust particles pointing away from the Sun.

dwarf planet (DWAHRF PLA-net)
An object in space that looks and acts like a planet but is much smaller.

equator (ih-KWAY-tur)
An imaginary line drawn around a planet that is an equal distance from the north and south poles.

geologic history
(jee-uh-LAH-jik HIS-tuh-ree)
The history of a place or planet's rocks, crust, and other solid matter.

gravity (GRA-vuh-tee)
The force that causes objects to be attracted toward Earth's center or toward other physical bodies in space, such as stars, planets, and moons.

mass (MAS)
The quantity of matter in a physical body that causes it to have weight when acted upon by gravity.

meteoroids (MEE-tee-uh-roydz)
Small particles or fragments that have broken free from an asteroid.

molecules (MAH-lih-kyoolz)
Two or more atoms of chemical elements that are bonded together. For example, a water molecule is two hydrogen atoms and one oxygen atom bonded together.

molten (MOHL-ten)
Melted, or liquefied, by heat.

nebula (NEH-byuh-luh)
Massive clouds of dust and gas in outer space. Many nebulae are formed by the collapse of stars, releasing matter that may, over millions or billions of years, clump together to form new stars.

orbiting (OR-bih-ting)
Circling in a curved path around another object.

planet (PLA-net)
An object in space that is of a certain size and that orbits, or circles, a star.

solar panels (SOH-ler PA-nulz)
A number of photovoltaic solar cells joined together in flat panels that absorb the Sun's energy so it can be used as a source of power.

solar system (SOH-ler SIS-tem)
The Sun and everything that orbits around it, including planets and their moons, asteroids, meteors, and comets.

trajectory (truh-JEK-tuh-ree)
The path taken by a flying object, or an object being moved by forces.

WEBSITES

For web resources related to the subject of this book, go to: www.windmillbooks.com/weblinks and select this book's title.

33

READ MORE

Aguilar, David A. *13 Planets: The Latest View of the Solar System*. Des Moines, IA: National Geographic Children's Books, 2011.

Landau, Elaine. *Mercury*. A True Book. Danbury, CT: Children's Press, 2008.

Taylor-Butler, Christine. *Mercury*. Scholastic News Nonfiction Readers: Space Science. Danbury, CT: Children's Press, 2008.

INDEX